Dancing Bears

BOOK A

Hilary Burkard

& Tom Burkard

Stories illustrated by
Helen Dickson
& Ed McLachlan

First published 2001, The Promethean Trust
Second Edition (Revised) 2002, The Promethean Trust
Third Edition (Revised) 2004, Hilary Burkard
Fourth Edition (Revised) 2005, Hilary Burkard
Fifth Edition (Revised) 2006, Hilary Burkard
Sixth Edition (Revised) 2012, Hilary Burkard
Seventh Edition (Revised) 2021, Hilary Burkard

Tracing exercises produced using *Handwriting For Windows*
available from: www.kber.co.uk

ISBN: 9781905174508

PUBLISHED BY HILARY BURKARD

DISTRIBUTED BY
SOUND FOUNDATIONS
www.soundfoundations.co.uk
mckenzie@soundfoundations.co.uk

Dancing Bears

Contents:

The Ground Rules:

The Sound Foundations philosophy:

As a teacher, your objective is to get your pupil to make the maximum number of correct responses—*and* the fewest errors—in the available time. If you manage to do this, you can't go far wrong.

1. **Teach—don't test.** Whenever a child gets stuck, say the sounds for them or tell them the word. Do not force them to 'work it out for themselves'. You do not want to make reading into a struggle.

2. Do not give ticks for a 'good try'. Just practise it and go back to it the next day.

3. Keep the lesson going at a cracking pace! Do not let your pupil's attention wander.

4. Daily lessons are essential. You only need to find 10 minutes per day for each slow reader.

The Teaching Techniques:

1. **Using the flashcards**—it is not enough just to 'know' the letter-sounds. The response must be instant and automatic. Practise the flashcards *every* lesson while using **Dancing Bears**!

2. **Using the cursor**—This is quite easy to learn. The cursor trains the child to read from left to right, and it trains them to look at every letter in a word.

3. **The 'Flashback Technique'**—After you have corrected an error, you must return to the same item again.

All this is explained on the following pages. Please read them carefully.

The Flashcards—it is not enough for pupils just to 'know' the letter-sounds. If the response is not instant and automatic, your pupil will not be able to concentrate on sounding out words. You must practise the flashcards *every* lesson while using Dancing Bears!

There are two sets of flashcards. Start teaching the green, Basic Flashcards straight away. Start introducing the blue Advanced Flashcards after page 72. Some of the blue cards represent two phonemes (eg, 'oke and ake'), but you will model these without breaking them down. All of the flashcards are numbered on the back; it is important to teach them in order—the lowest number first.

Getting started—First, you must find out which sounds your pupil already knows. Cut up the Basic Flashcards and show them to your pupil one at a time. Ask what sound each letter makes. If they give the letter name, say

"That's the *name* of the letter. What *sound* does it make?"

Once your pupil has missed five in a row, it is best to stop. Put all the cards they know in the pocket inside the front cover of the book. Put the rest in the pocket inside the back cover, keep them in order.

Daily revision:

At the beginning of each lesson, go through all the cards in the front pocket. As the pupil gets each one right place it in a pile in front of them.

If they make a mistake or have forgotten a sound, use the **Flashback Technique**:

- tell your pupil the right sound,
- ask them to repeat it,
- slip the card behind the next one.

When the card comes up again they will almost certainly get it right and you will have converted an error into a success.

Shuffle the cards to mix up the order before you put them away.

Introducing a new sound:

If your pupil has made no more than two errors when going through the cards, you can introduce a new one.

- Pick out three flashcards that the pupil already knows well. They should not sound or look like the letter you are introducing—for instance, you would never use the letter /t/ when introducing /d/, or /n/ when introducing /u/.

- From the cards that your pupil does not know, pick out the one with the lowest number. You will work with these four cards.

- Hold up the new card and tell your pupil the sound, make sure they repeat it correctly. If they have a speech impedement, make sure that they pronounce it as they would in a word.

- Slip the new card one card back. Show them the next card then put it to the back of the pack. The new card is now back on top. Repeat this a couple of times. Do this again, this time slipping the new card in two cards back each time it comes up. Your pupil has to remember it for a little bit longer. The old cards still go to the back each time. Repeat this a few times then finally put the new card at the back of the pack and go through the cards a couple of times more.

Your pupil may forget the new sound the next time you do your daily revision. However, by using the flashback technique, they will almost always start getting it right in a day or two—*it really is that easy!*

When do I stop using the flashcards?

When your pupil can say the sounds quicker than you can flip the flashcards then, unless they have not reached the page introducing that sound in the book, you can stop practising those cards. Do not be tempted to stop using the flashcards too soon. Your pupil must be able to respond instantly and automatically to the flashcards, otherwise, they will have trouble blending. You must practise 'past the point of perfection.' And no—your pupils will not get bored; children love getting it right!

The cards can be downloaded as a free PDF from:
https://www.soundfoundations.co.uk

Using the cursor:

The cursor is a piece of card about the size of a business card with a small notch cut out of one corner. You must use the cursor at all times.

- When your pupil is sounding out a word, you can reveal one sound at a time. For example, the word *shark* has three sounds— *sh...ar...k.*

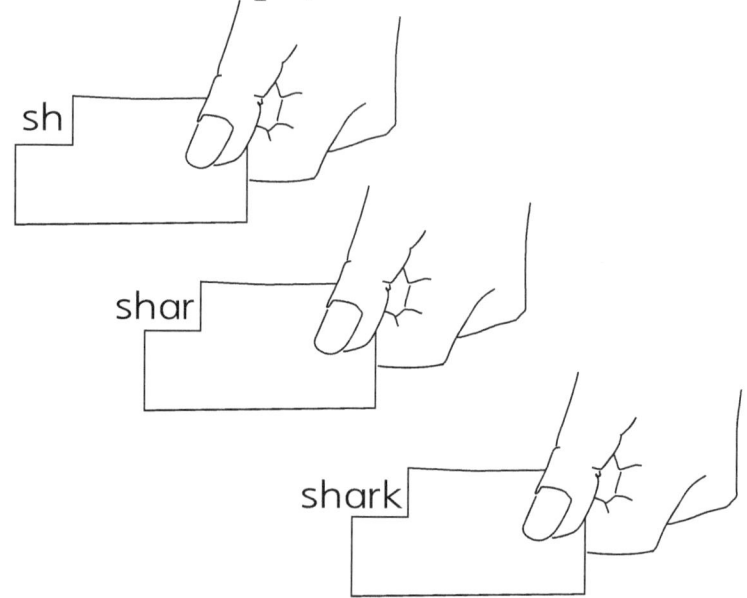

- When your pupil already knows a word, just move the cursor smoothly and quickly across the letters. Never sound out words if you don't have to!

- If your pupil makes a mistake, you can back up the cursor and then sound out the word.

The cursor eliminates visual confusion. When children have been taught to read whole words, their eyes often jump all over the place, trying to scramble the letters to make a 'fit' with a word they know. If you use the cursor, it is highly unlikely that your pupil will need coloured overlays or tinted glasses.

The Flashback Technique:

Use the Flashback Technique every time your pupil makes an error. If you go back to the instructions for using the flashcards, you will see that when they have forgotten a card, you tell them what it is and then put it behind the next card. That way the card comes up again while it is still fresh in their memory. This is an example of the Flashback Technique.

You will also use the Flashback Technique when your pupil is reading words. Whenever they fail to read the word correctly:

- model the word,
- get them to repeat it,
- go on to the next item,
- go back to the one they just missed,
- when you have finished a line, go back again to any words missed,
- when you have finished the exercise for the day, go back over all the missed words again.

This way, your pupil will usually earn their tick for the line the next day. (Remember—you never tick a line when the pupil gets it right on the second go—you must wait until the next lesson.)

Comprehension:

The main purpose of this book is to teach decoding, but it is also important for pupils to extend their vocabulary, and to understand what they have read. The Cloze exercises require pupils to pay attention to meaning in order to identify the missing word. Our stories provide valuable decoding practice and improve reading fluency. Some of the words in the stories may be unfamiliar to your pupil. If they ask the meaning of a word while reading, simply write it down where you see this symbol; ⌒. You can also write down any new words here. Discuss their meanings briefly at the end of the lesson, and ask if your pupil can think of any **synonyms** —other words with the same meaning. At the start of the next lesson, quickly review these words to check that your pupil has retained their new vocabulary (but never allow the discussion of meaning to become a distraction from reading practice!)

The Teaching Environment:

Always teach your pupil in a quiet room with no distractions. Never let them bring toys or mobile phones with them. Always sit facing your pupil. It is very difficult to use the cursor effectively if you are sitting side-by-side. You need eye contact. When you are facing your pupil it is easier to see when they are confused or getting tired. You can step in right away and show them what to do before they make a mistake and lose confidence.

Decoding Power Pages:

These exercises are the 'secret ingredient' of **Dancing Bears**. All good readers can decode letters to sound, even if they have never seen the word before. This is how good readers learn new words.

When children read the words on the Decoding Power Pages, they should not be trying to find a 'match' with a word they know. All the words on Decoding Power Pages are regular—they can all be 'sounded out' without any guesswork. Some of the words are very unusual, like 'quern', 'bort' and 'loach'—but they are all real words.

Remember—you must always use the cursor. You must teach pupils to scan from left to right and to read every sound.

Do not give a tick for a 'good try'. Your pupil must get all the words on a line right, without any help, to earn a tick. If you think they will be able to get it right on their own, you can back up the cursor and let them try again, but do not let them struggle or guess. If they have forgotten the sounds or are unable to blend them, say the sounds yourself and let them say the word. If they are in a total muddle, model the whole process and then get them to repeat it. Always go back to any word you helped with—see **The Flashback Technique** on page 8.

If your pupil makes a mistake, back up the cursor and sound out the word.

cat	tell	jet	cop	☐
sell	leg	hog	van	☐
mop	hen	nod	lip	☐
pit	off	bug	cab	☐
hot	till	job	men	☐
pin	set	can	egg	☐
did	mess	puff	hill	☐
has	yet	box	bun	☐
cut	bit	beg	gut	☐
dot	fog	sub	jazz	☐

Multi-sensory boxes—First, pupils trace the letters, saying the sound (or word) as they write it. Next, pupils read what they have traced.

ee   ar   sh

Using the cursor with digraphs—always reveal both letters at once.

s<u>ee</u>   s<u>ee</u>m   c<u>ar</u>   c<u>ar</u>t   ☐

<u>sh</u>op   wi<u>sh</u>   m<u>ee</u>t   n<u>ee</u>d   ☐

h<u>ar</u>d   di<u>sh</u>   p<u>ar</u>k   k<u>ee</u>p   ☐

I   the   I   the

Pupils must read the sentence, trace it, and then read it again.
They must say the words as they trace them.

I will get the dog.   ☐
I will get the dog.   ☐

Will I meet him?   ☐
Will I meet him?   ☐

Jim can keep a fish.   ☐
Jim can keep a fish.   ☐

ee   ar   sh

Using the cursor with digraphs—always reveal both letters at once.

see   seen   car   card   ☐

ship   fish   been   feet   ☐

hard   deep   part   keep   ☐

I   the   I   the

Can I see the card?   ☐

I can see the car.   ☐

I need the big box.   ☐

Can I keep it?   ☐

I wish I had a cat.   ☐

Max is in the shop.   ☐

The Bear Market:

These little dialogues can be used in many different ways—and you can invent your own. Like all of our stories, they should be regarded as enjoyment—pupils do not need to get ticks. Here are a few suggestions:

• The easiest way—especially with pupils who need more support—is for the teacher to read the first part, asking the questions, and the pupil to reply.

• As with other sentence-reading exercises, it is usually best for pupils to read a line first for accuracy, sounding out each word if necessary, and secondly for fluency. Always use the cursor.

• Pupils can also re-read the passages on successive days to improve accuracy and fluency.

• More confident pupils can read both parts—perhaps even adopting a different voice for each role.

• You can get two pupils together to read the different roles.

• You can even have pairs of pupils perform for the whole class—this will give them a real sense of achievement.

Bonus idea—

Children love 'Bear Markets', so why not end each session by going back to re-read one of their favourites? Let them colour in the pictures—in their own time, of course!

Pat: Did Tom get a dog?

Sam: Yes, Tom got a big dog.

Pat: Can Tom keep the dog?

Sam: Yes, Tom can keep his dog.

Pat: Will Jim feed his dog?

Sam: Yes, Jim will feed the dog.

Pat: Will the dog need a bed?

Sam: Yes, his dog will need a bed.

Pat: Can Jim pet the dog?

Sam: Yes, Jim can pet his dog.

Always use the cursor!

lot	vat	hill	lass	☐
see	seem	car	cart	☐
net	tax	ham	fit	☐
sat	jug	zap	met	☐
jam	pig	hut	tub	☐
shop	wish	meet	need	☐
six	tug	dad	zip	☐
gas	kiss	hum	miss	☐
hard	dish	park	keep	☐
fat	hit	dug	fin	☐

No no the

Ron: Did Mark dig the well?

Tam: Yes, Mark dug a deep well.

Ron: Did Josh see the well?

Tam: No, Josh fell in the well.

Ron: Did Josh get wet?

Tam: Yes, Josh got wet.

Ron: Will Josh feel bad?

Tam: No, Josh got in a hot tub.

Ron: Can Mark sit in the hot tub?

Tam: No, Mark can sit in the car.

| ee | ar | sh | th |

bar	barn	wi<u>th</u>	<u>th</u>is	☐
week	feed	<u>th</u>at	dark	☐
shut	Mark	shark	dish	☐

me you the me you the

Will you sit with me? ☐
Will you sit with me? ☐

Can you get that mop? ☐
Can you get that mop? ☐

Mark has a red car. ☐

I will get that dish. ☐

Did you feed this shark? ☐

Always use the cursor!

mat	bed	tag	log	☐
this	ship	barn	seem	☐
map	sip	boss	fix	☐
mud	tap	sum	big	☐
with	far	dish	feed	☐
fox	tan	get	nut	☐
pill	tip	dog	pop	☐
bud	ran	pub	lit	☐
that	card	weed	mash	☐
bet	yell	bat	mum	☐

ar th ck

far	farm	Jac<u>k</u>	du<u>ck</u>	☐
bath	teeth	thi<u>ck</u>	this	☐
path	Mi<u>ck</u>	shark	sharp	☐

he she he she

Did she see me? ☐
Did she see me? ☐

Will he feed this duck? ☐
Will he feed this duck? ☐

Did you run up the path? ☐

Jack got in the bath. ☐

That shark has sharp teeth. ☐

20

she he you

If your pupil reads a sentence slowly, he should read it again.

Jack has a sheep farm. ☐

Can you see his sheep? ☐

He keeps his sheep in the barn. ☐

Jess has a fish shop. ☐

She will sell me a fish. ☐

Will she cut up this fish? ☐

This car will not run. ☐

Can Ben fix this car? ☐

He can park the car in the barn. ☐

Did Mick feed the shark? ☐

DECODING ⚡ POWER ⚡ PAGE

Some of these words are unusual but they are all real words.

rod	box	cot	bill	☐
thick	Mark	teeth	shark	☐
top	rat	lap	rip	☐
jog	nap	rut	dip	☐
fan	fuzz	bus	doll	☐
rush	pack	far	thin	☐
hid	pin	not	hat	☐
posh	card	sheep	part	☐
dig	bag	lad	mid	☐
kid	pan	hop	let	☐

Mastery Test

If your pupil does not pass this test, they must go back to page 11. This is very important—a child who is struggling will not be learning. Contrary to what you would think, most children would rather go back than carry on getting things wrong. If your pupil needs to go back, use a different coloured pencil for ticking the boxes.

Use the cursor as you would on a Fluency Reading page.

Timed reading: 'Pass' mark is 15 seconds per line.

leg   kid   mix   fun   ☐

wet   van   job   yes   ☐

rag   fox   zip   cat   ☐

Reading accuracy: Pass mark is one mistake.
Do not prompt. You may allow the pupil to self correct, but you cannot say anything except "Try again".

Can you see the car?   ☐

She has sharp teeth.   ☐

Will he get a job?   ☐

I wish I had a dog.   ☐

Did Max need a bath?   ☐

he she me

Beth: If you need cash, you can get a job.

Mick: Did Jack get a job?

Sam: Yes, he got a job at the fish shop.

Beth: Did Jack sell you a fish?

Sam: No, he did not sell me a fish.

Mick: Will he sell me a cod fish?

Sam: No, but he will sell you a carp.

Beth: Did Jack get mad at his boss?

Mick: Yes, he hit him with a wet fish.

Beth: Did Jack get the sack?

Sam: You bet he got the sack!

Some of these words are unusual but they are all real words.

bad	hip	kin	yes	☐
bee	shop	car	wish	☐
bell	him	less	fed	☐
web	cup	fuss	ebb	☐
back	thick	lock	then	☐
ken	pun	wed	bill	☐
need	farm	meet	dark	☐
hiss	Ben	ell	kit	☐
luck	than	Beth	neck	☐
rap	wig	boff	huss	☐

er ck th

her	herd	Beth	Jack	☐
duck	Vern	sick	that	☐
kerb	Herb	thin	nerd	☐

my why my why

Beth has a herd of sheep. ☐

Will you tell my dad? ☐

Why is Jack sick? ☐

Vern sat on the kerb. ☐

Herb will get my duck. ☐

Has Beth fed my pig? ☐

Why did you hiss at Bert? ☐

Do not award ticks for a 'good try'—your pupil will pay for it later!

ship	keep	see	cash	☐
mix	ted	bid	fen	☐
jerk	that	tick	duck	☐
week	rush	bark	sheep	☐
bib	fad	luff	Jess	☐
herd	than	with	Bert	☐
hard	posh	been	sham	☐
wax	moss	con	got	☐
back	deck	thin	Herb	☐
part	mash	deep	far	☐

Cloze Sentences:

Pupils enjoy these exercises and they get to practise using the words they have learnt by reading them in meaningful sentences.

In the box at the top of each page, you will find the new words that your pupil will need in order to read the sentences. Most are exception (tricky) words or words with ambiguous digraphs. Move the cursor smoothly across the letters while saying the sounds in the word. If your pupil gets confused, point out which sounds are regular and which are tricky. If they cannot read the word, model the correct response, then use the Flashback Technique (see page 9) and repeat each word until firm.

Reading the sentences:

For this exercise you will need a blank sheet of thin card about A6 in size. Cover the sentence and ask the pupil to read the three 'answer' words above the sentence first, using the cursor as usual. (This is to prevent them from guessing at the missing word.) Then let them read the sentence, still using the cursor. If the pupil reads the sentence and selects the right answer without prompting, circle the correct word. (The pupil **should not** write the word—this takes too long and is a distraction.) Otherwise, the sentence should be repeated in a subsequent lesson. If the pupil does not know the meaning of a word, explain it as simply as possible—but never encourage pupils to guess at words they have read incorrectly.

Always use the cursor!

hen   bat   van

I am in a ___.

jug   rug   bell

We will sit on a ___.

pet   hop   lit

She did not let me get a ___.

hat   cup   dad

He did not tell his ___.

dud   mum   did

Did he miss his ___?

jug   hill   pit

Can a fat man dig a big ___?

hard   feel   farm   dish   □

Bart   mash   yard   weeds   □

shark   seeds   Josh   seen   □

Why is that shark sad?   □

Has she seen my seeds?   □

Bart has hit her car.   □

I will cut the weeds in the yard.   □

Why did Josh feel sick?   □

Shall I mix my dish of mash?   □

We had a hard job at the farm.   □

Tim, the Dim Cop.

Tim, the dim cop has a dog. Max is his dog.

Max said, "I need a fish. A big fish on a dish.

Can I get a fish?"

Tim said, "Why not? Yes, you can get a fish.

A big wet fish! Jess has a fish shop. We can

run by her fish shop in this car."

Tim, the dim cop got

in the car. Max got in

the cop car. But the

car did not run. Max

said, "We need gas in

this car!"

⌒⊃ ....

....

Some of these words are unusual but they are all real words.

buff	ness	bin	fib	☐
buck	sock	them	her	☐
fee	shot	feet	carp	☐
nag	teg	doff	cox	☐
bath	herb	kick	ruck	☐
dish	seem	card	lash	☐
tod	duff	will	fid	☐
puck	berth	dock	then	☐
peel	arm	shell	seed	☐
had	fell	sad	rug	☐

Remember to practise the flashcards at least once a day!

I bet a fat dog is well ___.

cat   fed   ham

A bad kid hit his ___.

nod   hug   dad

She did not let me on the ___.

bus   nut   kit

Get the dog off the ___.

gas   bed   pin

Can you get the lid off the ___?

bug   pig   jam

The mad dog bit the man on his ___.

hop   leg   tub

or ch qu Qu				

f<u>or</u>　　　f<u>or</u>k　　　<u>qu</u>ack　　　<u>t</u><u>or</u><u>ch</u>　　　☐

mu<u>ch</u>　　　<u>qu</u>it　　　<u>ch</u>ips　　　<u>qu</u>iz　　　☐

ri<u>ch</u>　　　<u>Qu</u>een　　　n<u>or</u>th　　　<u>qu</u>ick　　　☐

and why fly

The Queen has had my fish and chips.　☐

Did he get much for his car?　☐

Why did that duck quack?　☐

My dad has quit his job.　☐

You can get my torch if it is dark.　☐

We will fly up north this week.　☐

You will not get rich in this quiz.　☐

by   to   ch

Rich: Shall we run up to the park?

Merl: No, we can get a bus.

Rich: If you do not jog with me, you will get fat.

Jack: Can we run by the chip shop?

Merl: Yes, then we can get fish and chips.

Jack: We can feed them to the ducks in the park.

Rich: Can you see the hen with her chick?

Merl: Why did you let her get my chips?

Jack: She will not get fat—she will feed her chick.

Merl: But I need my chips!

Jack: Then you can run back to the chip shop.

Rich: Merl will not run if he can get a bus.

Do not award ticks for a 'good try'—your pupil will pay for it later!

fern	moth	thick	pack	☐
quack	fork	quit	much	☐
jar	bash	lee	shin	☐
lag	rid	wit	bob	☐
verb	thug	path	wack	☐
queen	North	chock	torn	☐
heel	art	shall	park	☐
cos	god	nib	ten	☐
York	larch	quiz	porch	☐
vat	ham	met	fit	☐

Mastery Test

If your pupil does not pass this test, they must go back to page 24. This is very important—a child who is struggling will not be learning. Contrary to what you would think, most children would rather go back than carry on getting things wrong. If your pupil needs to go back, use a different coloured pencil for ticking the boxes.

Use the cursor as you would on a Fluency Reading page.

Timed reading: 'Pass' mark is 15 seconds per line.

park	keep	this	shop	☐
with	sharp	her	sick	☐
need	will	dish	thin	☐

Reading accuracy: Pass mark is one mistake.

Do not prompt. You may allow the pupil to self correct, but you cannot say anything except "Try again".

Why is she in my car? ☐

Jack said that we can sit on the bed. ☐

Tell me why you did that. ☐

Did Bart cut the weeds in the back yard? ☐

Kim has a bad rash on her neck. ☐

The Pork Chop.

Tim, the dim cop said, "We need to get gas. We can not get to the fish shop if we need gas. Who can get the gas?"

Max said, "Yes, I can do that. My pal Vern has a can. I will see Vern, and then we can get the gas." Tim, the dim cop said, "Why not?"

Max ran to get his pal Vern. But then he met Herb, who had a big pork chop. Max said, "Will you sell me that pork chop?"

Will Max

get the gas?

you by my why try

map   dog   wet

She has not fed the ___.

boss   ham   mud

Can you cut the fat off my ___?

jam   gum   lap

My cat will sit on my ___.

din   box   gap

Can you rip the top off the ___?

fell   tag   bed

She has a rag doll by the ___.

jot   cap   gull

Why did she try on my ___?

er	ck	th

her	Herb	them	jack	☐
perk	luck	Nick	Beth	☐
socks	Rick	Vern	this	☐

give	have	live

Did Nick give them his socks? ☐

Do you have her torch? ☐

Herb and Beth live on a ship. ☐

Jack will perk up if she gives him a fish. ☐

Who will have bad luck this week? ☐

Did Vern give my chips to Rick? ☐

She did not have much beef. ☐

quick	rich	sort	charm	☐
Dick	kerb	Thor	Perth	☐
bar	seen	rash	darn	☐
quid	porch	quiff	forth	☐
Jack	perm	teeth	thorn	☐
cuff	bod	hem	nub	☐
worn	chap	quin	nor	☐
tern	pith	lick	chuck	☐
feed	cart	shun	mark	☐
lot	zap	tax	tub	☐

to who give

Meg: If we nag my mum, she will give us that horse.

Rod: My, this is a big horse.

Nick: Let us get up on her back.

Rod: I will give this horse a kick then she will run.

Meg: My, this horse is quick!

Nick: This horse is mad—Rod is a bad lad!

Meg: Who can get us off this horse?

Rod: If he is quick, my dad can get us off this horse.

Nick: Is he as quick as this horse?

Rod: See my dad run!

Meg: No! He fell in a well!

Nick: Duck! This horse will run in that barn!

by my why fly try

pig   hat   mug

Can I try on the red ___?

me   in   up

My dog will sit by ___.

dog   nap   cup

Can you fill my ___?

bee   jet   hen

Will you fly in a ___?

log   pan   bed

Why is she in ___?

egg   sun   box

Will the hen let me get an ___?

t<u>oy</u>	h<u>ay</u>	b<u>oy</u>	m<u>ay</u>	☐
p<u>ay</u>	R<u>oy</u>	R<u>ay</u>	torch	☐
s<u>ay</u>	short	w<u>ay</u>	s<u>oy</u>	☐

to do give have

May we feed the hay to the sheep? ☐

This path is the way to the farm. ☐

Roy gave his toys to Vern. ☐

Can you give me the soy in that jar? ☐

Who will pay for my fish and chips? ☐

Why did the boy say that? ☐

Do you need a torch to see in the dark? ☐

Always use the cursor!

weep	shim	weed	darn	☐
boy	say	day	joy	☐
goth	hers	shock	them	☐
tort	quill	perch	chub	☐
Roy	pay	toy	lay	☐
posh	lard	beet	marsh	☐
berg	hack	perk	thorn	☐
coy	soy	may	ray	☐
chick	quell	torch	ford	☐
hill	lass	net	jug	☐

my why try fly cry

dog   dad   ham

You can cut a bit off my ___.

wax   fish   web

Try not to let the cat get at my ___?

him   fog   hop

Why will he cry if we hit ___?

hop   yell   try

You can fly if you ___.

mess   rip   van

Why did Dad sell his red ___?

cry   hiss   cap

If you get mud on me, I will ___.

Max's Shorts.

Herb said to Max, "Why yes, I will sell you this pork chop. Give me six rats and you can have it."

Max said, "I do not have six rats, but I can give you my shorts. I have had a bath this week, so my shorts are not so bad."

Herb said, "I do not need the shorts. But you are a dog, so you can get six rats. Then you can have this pork chop."

Mastery Test

If your pupil does not pass this test, they must go back to page 40. This is very important—a child who is struggling will not be learning. Contrary to what you would think, most children would rather go back than carry on getting things wrong. If your pupil needs to go back, use a different coloured pencil for ticking the boxes.

Use the cursor as you would on a Fluency Reading page.

Timed reading: 'Pass' mark is 15 seconds per line.

boy	torch	Beth	quit	☐
say	queen	fork	chop	☐
way	much	luck	north	☐

Reading accuracy: Pass mark is one mistake.

Do not prompt. You may allow the pupil to self correct, but you cannot say anything except "Try again".

I need to give my toys to Mark. ☐

If you are quick, you may feed the shark. ☐

Do you have to pay for the fish and chips? ☐

Roy had to go to the farm in the dark. ☐

Why did you pay so much for that lock? ☐

or qu ai

l<u>ai</u>d	corn	quit	G<u>ai</u>l	☐
p<u>ai</u>d	f<u>ai</u>l	for	r<u>ai</u>n	☐
Queen	Norm	w<u>ai</u>t	quick	☐

to + day = today
for + got = forgot
can + not = cannot ☐

Pupils trace these words sums and then read them. Explain what they have to do, but do not award a tick unless they can read all of the words without prompting.

Has the Queen paid for her corn?   ☐

That hen laid an egg today.   ☐

I forgot to pay for my toys.   ☐

Why did Norm quit his job at the jail?   ☐

Gail cannot wait for her bus today.   ☐

If you are quick, you can see the Queen. ☐

Always use the cursor!

say	pail	main	joy	☐
horse	parch	norm	quip	☐
rack	verse	lath	thud	☐
paid	path	lain	hay	☐
arch	form	quiff	morse	☐
ash	eel	mesh	reed	☐
way	maid	fail	coy	☐
quin	orb	leech	fort	☐
Bert	nerve	hock	thick	☐
jam	tug	hum	log	☐

so are to do who

sun   beg   dot

Why is it so hot in the ___?

fill   dad   zap

I will cry if you do not let me sit by __.

car   hid   heel

I wish I had a ___.

sheep   jar   fish

The seeds are in the ___.

carp   art   hard

Do not hit him so ___.

ship   shop   shark

Who shall we feed to the ___?

Six rats.

Max had to get six rats to pay for Herb's pork chop. Then he met Gail, who had a pail of cat's tails. Max said, "I need to get six rats. Do you have six rats?"

Gail said, "No, but six rats live in Norm's barn. Tim, Kim and Jim are short rats with fat tails. Ben, Ken and Len are fat rats with short tails."

Max said, "If this is the road to Norm's barn, I can get the rats. Then I can pay for Herb's pork chop!"

try so go ay

Norm: Can you see if Shep will fly?

Tom: Shep is a dog, and dogs do not fly.

Chuck: You can fly if you try!

Norm: If we try to give Shep a bath, then he will fly.

Tom: No, my dad will say we are bad lads if we do that.

Chuck: May I try to fly?

Norm: No way! You are so short that you can not fly.

Chuck: But my duck is short and she can fly.

Tom: You are not a duck.

Chuck: The Queen is short and she can fly in a jet.

Norm: You are not the Queen.

l<u>oa</u>d   <u>oi</u>l   Chuck   c<u>oa</u>t   ☐

c<u>oi</u>n   l<u>oa</u>f   b<u>oa</u>t   chat   ☐

l<u>oa</u>n   j<u>oi</u>n   J<u>oa</u>n   b<u>oi</u>l   ☐

who do

sail + boat = sailboat

Will you join us for a quick chat?   ☐

Did you see who got my coat?   ☐

Chuck's car needs gas and oil.   ☐

That is not the way to load a gun.   ☐

Joan can boil the chips in oil.   ☐

Who will join me on my sailboat?   ☐

If you loan me the coins, I will get a loaf.   ☐

Remember to practise the flashcards at least once a day!

vain	soap	coin	bay	☐
pig	meet	zip	shop	☐
lark	jeep	harsh	shut	☐
foil	goal	may	Roy	☐
hut	need	six	kiss	☐
pert	mock	terse	chock	☐
fail	coach	pay	toil	☐
dad	gas	dish	tag	☐
cord	beech	quack	march	☐
miss	park	bed	keep	☐

Ken, the Tin Rat.

Max ran up the road to Norm's barn. Then he met Ken. Ken was a toy rat. Max said, "Who are you? You are not a fat rat with a short tail."

Ken said, "No, I am a tin rat. I am Ken, the tin rat. I live with Jill, my pet toad. She will boil the oil, and then we can have lunch."

"But Gail said that six rats live in Norm's barn," Max said. I cannot see Len and Ben, nor do I see Tim, Kim or Jim."

Ken said, "Len and Ben had to go to get the soap for Bill the goat. Tim, Kim and Jim had to go with them. Did you see them go in the sailboat?"

no go so are to do who

bee   car   wish

Will we go in the ___?

seem   bark   shop

Did she shut up the ___?

arm   ship   see

I had a red rash on my ___.

heel   shut   jar

I keep my pet fish in a ___.

sheep   dish   car

Can you see who is in the ___?

bat   bar   bed

Do not get the sheet off the ___.

DECODING ⚡ POWER ⚡ PAGE

Some of these words are unusual but they are all real words.

hard	mat	cart	boss	☐
coal	lay	nail	quoin	☐
harp	dosh	seep	par	☐
fix	with	barn	tap	☐
coil	oak	Tay	waif	☐
therm	serve	lock	wick	☐
sum	dish	fox	mash	☐
oil	poach	soy	lain	☐
shorn	Norse	cheek	quid	☐
mat	ship	feed	tag	☐

no go so are to do who

dish   fish   feet

Did he try to reel in the big ____?

bash   bee   ship

Has she been on a ____?

sheep   cash   bar

Who can feed the ____?

fee   ash   car

Did my dog bark at the ____?

shell   char   feed

I cut my shin on a sharp ____.

jar   feet   hut

Why has the cat got mud on his ____?

Mastery Test

If your pupil does not pass this test, they must go back to page 53. This is very important—a child who is struggling will not be learning. Contrary to what you would think, most children would rather go back than carry on getting things wrong. If your pupil needs to go back, use a different coloured pencil for ticking the boxes.

Use the cursor as you would on a Fluency Reading page.

Timed reading: 'Pass' mark is 15 seconds per line.

wait	road	sail	corn	☐
rack	join	boat	rain	☐
tail	oil	path	Vern	☐

Reading accuracy: Pass mark is one mistake.
Do not prompt. You may allow the pupil to self correct, but you cannot say anything except "Try again".

Did you see who paid for the coach? ☐

Get the soap and have a soak in the bath. ☐

Gail's pet goat had to wait for her lunch. ☐

Will you loan me a coin for my chips? ☐

Norm will join us for a run in the park. ☐

do oy ay

Roy:	The Queen said that she will quit her job today.
Nell:	Why did she say that?
Queen:	It is a hard job but the pay is not so bad.
Roy:	Do you have a lot to do?
Queen:	I have to feed my dogs and give my horse her hay.
Nell:	Who will be the Queen?
Roy:	Can I be the Queen?
Nell:	No, you are a boy. A boy can not be Queen.
Roy:	Can my mum be Queen?
Queen:	Your mum has a hard job—she has a boy.
Nell:	Then I will be Queen!

rain	Roy	lay	paid	☐
way	wait	Kay	boy	☐
toy	Gail	sail	say	☐

tin + foil = tinfoil
sail + boat = sailboat

Kay and the boys are on the way to the jail. ☐

If it rains, her coat will get wet. ☐

Why did you wait for the coach? ☐

My goat had tinfoil for lunch. ☐

My dad got me a toy sailboat. ☐

Did Gail say who has the soap? ☐

Roy lay in bed today, so he will not get paid. ☐

Some of these words are unusual but they are all real words.

bed	this	log	seem	☐
quern	thick	erse	thug	☐
bait	foam	Hoy	quail	☐
morn	queen	chard	gorse	☐
reel	marl	hash	sharp	☐
map	far	sip	thus	☐
check	herl	lack	with	☐
tail	day	foal	soil	☐
cork	chart	quiz	lord	☐
pill	ran	weed	rug	☐

Advanced Flashcards:

The blue Advanced Flashcards should be cut up and used in just the same way as the Basic Flashcards. Some of these cards represent two phonemes (eg, 'oke and ake'). Your pupil will already be familiar with words such as *give* and *horse*, that end in silent 'e', but this is the first introduction to the Split Digraph or Magic 'E' Rule. Model the sounds without breaking them down. There is no need to explain the rule unless your pupil is really confused by the silent 'e'.

Final Consonant Blends:

Most children will master consonant blends easily with the help of the following sheets.

You will notice that the words are arranged in pairs. The first is a CVC word and the second is the same word with another consonant added. The first pair is:

ten   tent

By now your pupil will be able to read 'ten' easily. They should be able to add the final consonant without too much difficulty but if they cannot, you will have to do a bit of oral blending for them. For instance, say the word 'ten'—pause, then add the final /t/. Then ask them what the word is. Obviously, you do not give them a tick until they can do this entirely on their own.

Final Consonant Blends

Always use the cursor!.

ten	tent	bus	bust	☐
tan	tank	pin	pink	☐
pass	past	loss	lost	☐
hill	hilt	ran	rant	☐
sun	sunk	chum	chump	☐
gun	gunk	sill	silk	☐
shell	shelf	hem	hemp	☐
dam	damp	hell	held	☐
Bess	best	well	Welsh	☐

No Lunch for Max.

Max had to wait for the rest of the tin rats. They got back the next day. Max said, "We must go to see Herb, who has a pork chop for my lunch. He said that he needs six rats."

Ken, Len and Ben went up the road with Max. So did Jim, Kim and Tim. They went up the road to see Herb.

Max said, "I have six rats for you. Can I have that pork chop? I need my lunch."

Herb was mad. He said, "Why, they are just tin rats. I need fat rats with short tails. I need short rats with fat tails. But I do not need toy rats."

Max said, "Then I must get Vern, who has a gas can. Then I can get the gas. Then I can go in the car with Tim, the dim cop. We can go to see Jess, who has a fish shop. Then I can have my lunch."

go was why to do who

heel   shed   arm

Why did he shut my dog in his ___?

fee   mark   pill

If I feel ill, who will get me a ___?

car   dash   seem

Who was hit by the red ___?

shark   feet   till

Why did the man in the shop keep his cash in the ___?

dash   dark   deed

It is hard to see a car in the ___.

shop   sharp   sheet

Do you need to go to the ___?

<u>air</u>	f<u>air</u>	w<u>ore</u>	b<u>eer</u>	☐
p<u>air</u>	s<u>oar</u>	d<u>eer</u>	sc<u>ore</u>	☐
ch<u>eer</u>	m<u>ore</u>	ch<u>air</u>	h<u>oar</u>d	☐

they of who

Sit her on that chair and I will cut her hair. ☐

Joan wore her red dress to the fair. ☐

I will give a cheer if they score a goal. ☐

Did you see that bat soar in the air? ☐

My dad has a hoard of coins in a box. ☐

Who will get more beer for the boys? ☐

Gail wore a pair of red socks today. ☐

DECODING ⚡ POWER ⚡ PAGE

Do not award ticks for a 'good try'—your pupil will pay for it later!

core	leer	chair	board	☐
bust	held	jump	land	☐
Kay	foil	loath	main	☐
yank	lamp	help	dent	☐
Norm	cheep	quip	born	☐
and	dunk	lend	silk	☐
shack	verve	oath	rock	☐
fist	tank	send	cost	☐
carve	deed	gash	reef	☐
pub	weed	pill	that	☐

Final Consonant Blends

hell	help	pan	pant	☐
loss	lost	ran	rank	☐
pun	punch	well	weld	☐
bus	busk	cull	cult	☐
lass	last	miss	mist	☐
gull	gulf	gas	gasp	☐
less	lest	ten	tend	☐
gull	gulp	fun	funk	☐
mass	mask	bell	belt	☐

Joan, the Big Roan.

Ken the tin rat felt sad, for Max was in a bad way. Big dogs need to have lunch. Ken said, "I will loan you my horse. Joan the big roan can get you to Jess's fish shop. Then you can have lunch."

Max said, "Why, thank you. A fish on a dish will hit the spot." So Max got on Joan the big roan, and they went off to get some fish.

On the way to the fish shop, they met Tim the dim cop. Tim was in his cop car. He had to sleep in his car, and his hair was a mess.

Tim was glad to see Max. He got on Joan the big roan, and off they went to the fish shop. But they forgot that it was Sunday.

"No!" Tim said. "Jess has shut her fish shop!"
But Joan said, "Do not be so sad. I have lots
of Mars bars in my nosh bag."

shop   barn   feet

Do you keep the sheep in the yard or in the ___?

art   far   cab

You need some cash to go in a ___.

pecks   socks   licks

Mum said I have to pick up my ___.

herd   sock   bath

She has a duck in her ___.

thick   shop   jerk

Have they been to the ___?

mark   herb   feet

My dog will try to lick my ___.

Mastery Test

If your pupil does not pass this test, they must go back to page 68. This is very important—a child who is struggling will not be learning. Contrary to what you would think, most children would rather go back than carry on getting things wrong. If your pupil needs to go back, use a different coloured pencil for ticking the boxes.

Use the cursor as you would on a Fluency Reading page.

Timed reading: 'Pass' mark is 15 seconds per line.

lost	belt	foil	quiz	☐
help	chart	pain	joy	☐
sank	herb	goat	hay	☐

Reading accuracy: Pass mark is one mistake.
Do not prompt. You may allow the pupil to self correct, but you cannot say anything except "Try again".

Have they had some of the punch? ☐

Do they have some beer on board that boat? ☐

Who can lend me a hand with this chair? ☐

Did that silk vest cost much? ☐

Faith and Vern live on the main road. ☐

Fluency Reading:

Timed readings will help your pupil read words quickly and automatically. At first, the times are very generous and most pupils will find them easy to acheive. However, some children get nervous when they are being tested, and you do not want them to be worried by the stopwatch. For real timing-phobics, sit the child with their back to a wall clock with a second hand.

Frame the first word in the line with the cursor, and then say 'go'. Move the cursor as fast as the pupil can read. Record the time on the sheet and tick the line off if the pupil reads every word within 10 seconds. The usual rules apply—if your pupil makes a mistake, you can move the cursor back and let them have another go but you cannot give them any help. Model any word they get stuck on and re-time that line the next day.

Unless your pupil is extremely slow, they will want to try for bonus points. You can award one bonus point if they read the line in 8 seconds, and two bonus points if they read it in 6 seconds. Motivate your pupil with rewards when they get enough points. If your pupil wants to have another go at a line, they must wait until the following day.

Story:

The purpose of the story is to provide decoding practice and to improve reading fluency, but you should always check your pupil's comprehension, and, at the end of the lesson, briefly discuss the meaning of any new or unfamiliar words. Write these down where you see this symbol: ⌂.

There are no tick-boxes for this exercise but, if your pupil struggles with a sentence, they should be encouraged to read it again. If their reading is very hesitant, it may be a good idea to read the story twice to improve fluency and comprehension. Model any words on which the pupil gets stuck.

gut	sell	mop	pit	□ ☆ ☆
hot	pin	did	has	□ ☆ ☆
cut	egg	leg	hen	□ ☆ ☆
off	till	set	mess	□ ☆ ☆
yet	bit	jet	hog	□ ☆ ☆
nod	bug	job	can	□ ☆ ☆
puff	box	beg	cop	□ ☆ ☆
van	lip	cab	men	□ ☆ ☆
tell	hill	bun	cat	□ ☆ ☆

On the Way to the shop.

Mark was lost. His mum had sent him to get a loaf and some milk for lunch. He went up the road to the shop and then he met Vern. Vern was a big boy and he had a pet snail.

"You must meet my snail." Vern said. "Froid is my pet snail. He has just had beer and roast beef for lunch. See him sit in his chair and rest."

Vern let Mark pick up Froid, who was Vern's pet snail. Vern let Mark pick up his chair.

"Froid has wet feet." said Mark.

Vern said, "Why, yes, Froid is a snail!"

Next, we will tell you why Mark got lost.

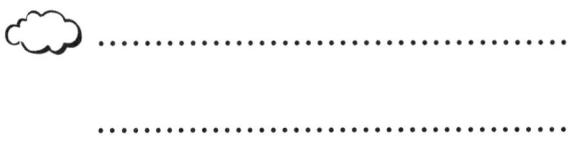

Remember to practise the flashcards at least once a day!

kip	null	yam	bun	□
mink	weld	risk	past	□
hair	fore	peer	boar	□
ant	sink	fond	daft	□
Joan	aim	roach	fay	□
barn	lush	sash	seek	□
pong	imp	lunch	went	□
nick	kerf	term	thug	□
worn	quench	chill	port	□
sand	punch	belt	end	□

rock   than   herd

Can he pick up that ___?

luck   fern   shop

They have some fish in that ___.

peck   feet   this

Do not run on the deck with wet ___.

with   car   seem

They can go in my ___.

moth   herd   sock

Can a bee fly as far as a ___?

pick   perk   park

Some of us will go to the ___.

where there
be + fore = before

Joan: My dad has a keen boat—it has a red sail.

Herb: Can we go and sail in his boat?

Joan: He said we must ask him before we go.

Rick: Where is he?

Joan: He has a job on the farm.

Herb: Can we go there and ask him?

Rick: Why not just go and sail in his boat?

Herb: Yes, we do not have to tell him!

Rick: There is the boat! Shall we get in?

Herb: Can I hoist the sail?

Rick: Away we go! This is fun!

Joan: Why are my socks so wet?

oi air eer ore

joint	pair	more	deer	☐
chair	queer	point	tore	☐
moist	wore	cheer	hair	☐

of where here there

We need some more chairs here. ☐

The coat she wore is moist with the rain. ☐

There are six deer in the park. ☐

Where did you get that pair of red socks? ☐

Can you point to the boy who tore his vest? ☐

You can sit in the chair if you feel a bit queer. ☐

There are six joints of pork left. ☐

Always use the cursor!

jail	soy	oat	quoit	☐
beer	more	fair	roar	☐
born	quilt	chip	for	☐
moist	wimp	hang	fact	☐
verve	teem	mush	hark	☐
shore	fair	board	deer	☐
chimp	bung	ramp	pink	☐
huff	bell	odd	lax	☐
think	erne	muck	chick	☐
serf	thank	pick	perch	☐

kerb   dish   luck

Nan said not to let the cat lick the ___.

pith   duck   week

She said she has had bad luck this ___.

sock   seek   sick

Do you feel ___?

duck   six   pith

They will have to rush to get back here by ___.

lick   lack   lock

They hid some of the cash in a box with a ___.

hat   ham   hop

Can you serve me with some thin cut ___?

dot	lot	net	sat	☐ ☆ ☆
jam	six	gas	wax	☐ ☆ ☆
dug	fog	vat	tax	☐ ☆ ☆
jug	pig	tug	kiss	☐ ☆ ☆
hit	got	sub	hill	☐ ☆ ☆
ham	zap	hut	dad	☐ ☆ ☆
hum	fat	had	jazz	☐ ☆ ☆
lass	fit	met	tub	☐ ☆ ☆
zip	miss	hex	fin	☐ ☆ ☆

Off to the Dump.

Mark let Vern have his pet snail back. Froid the snail just sat in his chair and Vern let him rest.

Vern said, "You must go to the dump with me. We can have lots of fun at the dump."

Mark said, "But I must go to the shop and get a loaf and some milk for my lunch. Mum will be cross if I am not back".

Vern said, "It will be quick if we fly. You can fly if you try!"

So Mark and Vern set off to fly to the dump. They got to the dump with Froid, the pet snail. The dump was big and it was full of junk. It had a pong of damp dog.

"We can have lots of fun in that hill of moist muck!" said Vern.

boar   board   faith   foam   ☐

quail   oak   sail   oars   ☐

soap   train   coarse   boat   ☐

card + board=cardboard
was here where

My toy train is here, in this cardboard box.   ☐

Mix that soap and it will foam up.   ☐

A boar is a pig that has tusks.   ☐

Where was the sailboat today?   ☐

Do goats have coarse hair?   ☐

Here is an oak board that will do for a shelf. ☐

The boat will not go if you forget the oars.   ☐

DECODING ⚡ POWER ⚡ PAGE

Do not award ticks for a 'good try'—your pupil will pay for it later!

joint	kiln	dump	song	☐
sore	pair	jeer	soar	☐
yarn	gosh	feel	teen	☐
chop	bort	quill	pork	☐
zest	gasp	melt	chink	☐
ore	lair	queer	roar	☐
win	gaff	Max	rig	☐
ring	quest	pelt	jilt	☐
load	coy	quail	void	☐
say	her	quill	coin	☐

Always use the cursor!

quit   quick   quack

Can a duck ___?

teem   thick   teeth

A shark has a lot of sharp ___.

quiz   card   cash

A rich man has a lot of ___.

mat   mug   mop

You can sit here on this ___.

cash   chill   chuck

Do they have much ___?

cheek   dish   chin

There are a lot of fish on my ___.

swim steer

Rick: This is a keen sailboat!

Herb: Yes, it is a fast boat. We can sail far away.

Joan: Did you feel a bump?

Rick: Yes, I think we just hit a rock.

Joan: That must be why my socks are wet.

Herb: I think this boat will sink!

Rick: You must steer for that bunch of weeds.

Joan: Yes, it will not be so deep there.

Herb: I cannot steer this boat.

Rick: I think we have just run onto a sand bank.

Herb: That is just as well. I am not a fish and I cannot swim.

Joan: I see my dad on the shore—do you think he will see us?

	Timed reading:			
☐ Pass: 10 sec.	☆ Bonus: 8 sec.	☆ Double Bonus: 6 sec.		

mat	map	mud	fox	☐ ☆ ☆
pill	bud	bet	dux	☐ ☆ ☆
kid	bed	sip	tap	☐ ☆ ☆
tan	tip	ran	yell	☐ ☆ ☆
fell	pan	tag	boss	☐ ☆ ☆

Bart, the Junk-Yard Dog.

So Mark, Vern and Froid went to the hill of moist muck. Froid was just a short snail, so he had to go. Then they met Bart, the junk-yard dog. Bart had the pong of a damp dog—but then Bart *was* a damp dog.

Bart said, "Will you join me for some roast toad? I have a pair of hot toads in my hill of moist muck."

Vern said, "Froid can not have roast toad for he is a snail. Can we have a short shark?"

Bart said, "The last short shark went off to see the Queen, but you can have a sharp shark."

Mark said, "Thank you so much, but I must tell my mum or she will be cross."

Mastery Test

If your pupil does not pass this test, they must go back to page 85. This is very important—a child who is struggling will not be learning. Contrary to what you would think, most children would rather go back than carry on getting things wrong. If your pupil needs to go back, use a different coloured pencil for ticking the boxes.

Use the cursor as you would on a Fluency Reading page

Timed reading: 'Pass' mark is 15 seconds per line.

more	bunch	coil	porch	☐
fair	damp	moat	kerb	☐
beer	melt	quail	point	☐

Reading accuracy: Pass mark is one mistake.
Do not prompt. You may allow the pupil to self correct, but you cannot say anything except "Try again".

Did you see where the sailboat went? ☐

A cardboard box will not keep you dry if it rains hard. ☐

Who was the boy in the torn coat? ☐

The coach to Perth will be here on Sunday. ☐

There is no more of that beef joint left. ☐

Initial Consonant Blends

Remember to practise the flashcards at least once a day!

stop	play	flag	☐
drop	glad	swim	☐
grab	spell	slip	☐
brick	clay	trick	☐
skill	black	crab	☐
frog	pram	twin	☐
snap	dwell	smug	☐
skim	Gwen	twill	☐

help + less = helpless
may + be = maybe
come some where there

Herb:	We cannot get back to shore— this boat is stuck.
Joan:	Maybe my dad will come and get us.
Joan's Dad:	Why not stay where you are? You can have so much fun!
Herb:	But we will starve if we are stuck here!
Joan's Dad:	You can boil some clams and frogs for lunch.
Joan:	But we need fish and chips!
Herb:	We need sweets and crisps!
Joan's Dad:	You can roast crabs and snails for snacks.

Herb: You cannot let us stay here! We are helpless kids!

Joan: You are my dad—you cannot let me stay here!

Joan's Dad: If you come back, I have lots of chores for you to do.

Joan: Dad! There are black bugs in my socks!

FLUENCY READING

Timed reading:

☐ Pass: 10 sec.   ☆ Bonus: 8 sec.   ☆ Double Bonus: 6 sec.

sum	get	dog	pub	☐ ☆ ☆
bat	sad	hop	log	☐ ☆ ☆
fix	big	nut	pop	☐ ☆ ☆
lit	mum	rug	let	☐ ☆ ☆
rod	top	jog	fan	☐ ☆ ☆

Shark Oil.

Mark went with Vern, Froid and Bart to the deep pond, where they met Herb. Herb was the sharp shark.

"I am glad you are here for lunch," he said. "My back is sore and I need some oil. Here is ten quid for some oil."

Bart said, "There are lots of junk cars here. I can go and drain some oil, then we can boil a joint of beef. I will bark if I get lost."

Then Froid fell off his chair in to some moist muck.

Vern said, "Can you see where Froid went?"

Mark said, "Yes, he is in his shell. Shall I go and get my loaf and some milk?"

But Bart was not back with the oil so they had to ask Herb to wait in the deep pond. It was dark in his shell so Froid went to sleep.

"Who will tell my mum where I am?" Asked Mark.

Always use the cursor!

bunch	elf	foist	bang	☐
frog	twin	still	snap	☐
oat	rail	hoist	bay	☐
clock	flag	pram	swim	☐
quell	horn	char	cord	☐
blot	droll	flock	grit	☐
lung	chunk	act	vest	☐
twill	slop	green	crab	☐
sheer	bore	fair	oar	☐
pail	quip	horse	joy	☐

luck   term   park

There are ten ducks in the ___.

porch   pick   port

Shut the dog in the ___.

park   fork   ford

Can I dig here with my ___?

cord   quell   chop

Where is my big, fat, pork ___?

chins   chips   chills

They had some fish and ___.

fork   port   torch

You can see in the dark if you have a ___.

air + port = airport
may + be = maybe
be + fore = before
some where there

Joan: Did you help Dad fix the sailboat?

Rick: Yes, it had a gash where we hit the rock.

Herb: We had to fix it with some bits of oak.

Joan: Let us go and play before my dad gives us some more chores.

Herb: I think it will rain. If we play in the sand, we will get wet.

Rick: Maybe we can go to Spain. There is no rain in Spain.

Herb: Yes! We must go to Spain! It is dry in Spain.

Joan: Ask that man the way to Spain.

Rick: He said you must fly to Spain in a jet.

Herb: You must go to the airport and get a jet to Spain.

Joan: Do you think my dad will get cross if we fly to Spain?

Rick: Where is the airport?

hid	dig	bad	bell	☐ ☆ ☆
hug	box	rat	nap	☐ ☆ ☆
fuzz	pin	bag	hip	☐ ☆ ☆
him	pot	cot	lap	☐ ☆ ☆
rut	bus	not	lad	☐ ☆ ☆

A Crock of Eels.

Mark and Vern left the deep pond to see where Bart had got to. Bart was a damp dog and damp dogs smell, so Mark and Vern just had to sniff. Herb the sharp shark had to stay in the deep pond for he did not have a bus pass. Froid was stuck in the moist muck, he still did not have his chair.

"I can smell a strong pong," said Vern, "so Bart must be here." But Bart was not here and he was not there.

Mark said, "Here is a crock of eels. They smell a lot. They must be the things we can smell."

Vern said, "Ask that eel if he has seen Bart, the junk-yard dog." But the eel did not say where Bart was. He just swam in his crock and stank.

Mark said, "I must get back or my mum will tell the cops that I am lost."

Initial Consonant Blends

fleet	storm	sleep	start	train	☐
float	creep	spoil	trail	cloth	☐
swim	Fred	bleed	play	clock	☐

saw come put
a + way = away
be + fore = before

I think Joan snores in her sleep. ☐

We saw them start off up the trail at six o'clock. ☐

Come here and play with my toy train. ☐

You will spoil that cloth if you bleed on it. ☐

Put the toys away and go to sleep. ☐

I saw Fred creep up on the deer. ☐

You must swim back to shore before the storm. ☐

Remember to practise the flashcards at least once a day!

prim	grab	drill	blob	☐
teeth	hush	chard	shark	☐
skid	glut	fled	class	☐
tuck	perch	maths	neck	☐
chat	ford	tore	quick	☐
clink	bluff	grass	plan	☐
moan	play	gait	coil	☐
lore	pair	oar	seer	☐
tuft	silk	ask	hump	☐
parch	fail	leech	hock	☐

some saw
air + port = airport
a + way = away

Joan: My dad has some more chores for us.

Herb: I have to put the trash in the bin.

Rick: I have to paint some chairs.

Herb: I have to help load some junk into the skip.

Joan: I have to help feed the sheep.

Rick: If we are quick, we can creep away.

Herb: Yes, we can go to the airport.

Joan: And we can fly to Spain!

Rick: It is hot in Spain, and we can play in the sand!

Herb: And we can swim in the bay!

Rick: Yes, we must go to the airport.

Joan: I think my Dad saw us creep away.

FLUENCY READING

kin	less	cup	bill	☐ ☆ ☆
rip	dip	doll	hat	☐ ☆ ☆
mid	yes	fed	gum	☐ ☆ ☆
add	bee	web	ken	☐ ☆ ☆
need	hiss	rap	ship	☐ ☆ ☆

Groyne, the Grey-Green Goat.

Who do you think Mark and Vern ran in to on the way to the hill of moist muck? They met Groyne, the grey-green goat, who wore his hair in a quiff.

Vern said, "My pal Mark needs to get a loaf and some milk for his mum. Is there a store in this dump?"

Groyne bit a chunk of brick and had a munch on some foil. Then he said, "You must ask Bart, the damp dog. I just have my lunch here."

Mark said, "We must go back to the deep pond and get Froid, the short snail. He must miss his chair."

Groyne, the grey-green goat, said, "You must not trust Herb, the sharp shark, for he has no bus pass."

So Vern paid Groyne six coins for his torch and they went back on the trail to the deep pond.

DECODING ⚡ POWER ⚡ PAGE

Do not award ticks for a 'good try'—your pupil will pay for it later!

crack	drip	glass	swig	☐
woad	joint	stay	laid	☐
chuck	verse	kith	peck	☐
grip	flop	clam	skill	☐
torch	corm	cheep	quit	☐
tart	josh	yard	beef	☐
pang	mend	nest	film	☐
more	beer	Claire	hoard	☐
loach	hay	loin	Cain	☐
punch	soy	quilt	long	☐

here where there

shop   short   such

Where is the path to the ___?

chop   torn   barn

The Queen was not born in a __.

sort   sock   such

She has torn her ___.

fort   form   fork

Try not to jab me with that sharp ___.

bed   chair   bath

I put my toy duck and some soap in the ___.

chat   chain   cheek

Come here and join us for a ___.

there where
air + port = airport
a + way = way
hand + cuffs = handcuffs

Herb: We are off to Spain!

Joan: But we have to get to the airport.

Herb: There is Tim, the dim cop. We can ask his dog, Max.

Joan: Yes, Tim is dim, so they give him a smart dog.

Max: Yes, that way Tim cannot get lost.

Herb: Where is the road to the airport?

Max: I can see that you are bad kids who have run away from your dad.

Joan: We are not bad kids—I am just fed up with my chores.

Max: Kids must have chores. That is the way it is.

Herb: You must help us get away!

Max: No, I cannot do that. I will bark if you run away.

Joan: Why has Tim got the handcuffs off his belt?

Mastery Test

If your pupil does not pass this test, they must go back to page 105. This is very important—a child who is struggling will not be learning. Contrary to what you would think, most children would rather go back than carry on getting things wrong. If your pupil needs to go back, use a different coloured pencil for ticking the boxes.

Use the cursor as you would on a Fluency Reading page

Timed reading: 'Pass' mark is 15 seconds per line.

spoil	store	green	black	☐
train	fair	free	play	☐
sweet	roar	smart	croak	☐

Reading accuracy: Pass mark is one mistake.
Do not prompt. You may allow the pupil to self correct, but you cannot say anything except "Try again".

Come here and we can play with the clay. ☐

We will try to get there before the storm comes. ☐

Where shall I put the green sweets? ☐

They saw us put the toys by the stairs. ☐

The stern is the back end of a ship. ☐

king	aft	bank	champ	☐
norm	chit	quilt	inch	☐
twig	fret	snip	plum	☐
Ark	meek	short	tosh	☐
elm	dung	mist	quench	☐
verse	sack	berth	luck	☐
flap	drop	bran	stab	☐
sheer	core	fair	boar	☐
foil	goad	boy	ail	☐
shelf	rung	pond	mint	☐

Timed reading:

☐ Pass: 10 sec.   ☆ Bonus: 8 sec.   ☆ Double Bonus: 6 sec.

dud	shop	rudd	pun	☐ ☆ ☆
farm	Ben	wig	rid	☐ ☆ ☆
keep	gig	jut	car	☐ ☆ ☆
fuss	wed	meet	ell	☐ ☆ ☆
boff	see	mix	pug	☐ ☆ ☆
wish	ebb	biff	dark	☐ ☆ ☆

Mark and the Shard.

Mark and Vern left Groyne, the grey-green goat, who wore his hair in a quiff, and went off on the trail back to the deep pond. On the way, Mark slid on some slick clay. He fell on a shard of glass and cut his arm.

Vern said, "I will put some mud on the cut so it will not bleed. It is not a bad cut and I think you will live."

Then they saw a damp dog come up the hill.

"It must be Bart," said Mark, "I can tell by the smell."

Bart said, "I live in that smart shack on the steep hill. Come up the stairs with me and I will give you some lunch."

Just then Mark saw Froid, the short snail. He had green paint on his shell and he was still stuck in the moist muck.

cab	coat	coy

Where did you put my ___?

coal	coat	coach

They will go to the fun-fair by __.

say	soil	sail

Come and see the boat with the red ___.

bay	bed	boil

The sick boy lay on the ___.

foam	farm	fail

We saw a goat at the ___.

laid	void	loaf

Have you paid the man for the ___?

Consonant Blends

scarf   shelf   sweet   point   ☐

free   moist   snarl   twerp   ☐

smart   green   stay   think   ☐

saw could your
rain + storm = rainstorm

I saw your scarf by the green chair.   ☐

If you are smart, you will stay away today. ☐

Could you tell your dog not to snarl?   ☐

The rainstorm has left the soil moist.   ☐

Could you point to the deer you saw?   ☐

That twerp thinks the sweets are free.   ☐

Could you put your torch back on the top   ☐
shelf?

could where put

Herb: And then Tim put us in jail!

Rick: And Max bit my hand!

Joan: I was so glad that Mum and Dad got us.

Herb: I will not be a bad kid—it is not so much fun.

Joan: And I will do my chores.

Herb: Where is that junk? I will load it in the skip.

Rick: Where is that chair? I will paint it.

Joan: Where are the sheep? I will feed them.

Herb: Where is that trash? I will put it in the bin.

Rick: So you see, we are not bad kids.

Joan: Do you think we could have some sweets?

Rick: Tell me, is it still hot and dry in Spain?

jail   join   jay

If you are bad, you may be put in ___.

pail   poach   pain

The boy will moan if he is in ___.

wait   week   woad

He said that he can come this ___.

roach   ray   road

We saw a bus come up the ___.

sheep   seeds   soaps

Dig the soil with a fork and put in the ___.

arm   egg   oath

Shall I poach you an ___?

Timed reading:

☐ Pass: 10 sec.   ☆ Bonus: 8 sec.   ☆ Double Bonus: 6 sec.

kit	huss	cash	Ted	☐ ☆ ☆
yon	jerk	week	bib	☐ ☆ ☆
herd	hard	den	back	☐ ☆ ☆
part	mitt	that	rush	☐ ☆ ☆
fad	than	posh	moss	☐ ☆ ☆
deck	mash	bid	tick	☐ ☆ ☆
bark	luff	with	been	☐ ☆ ☆
con	thin	deep	fen	☐ ☆ ☆
duck	sheep	Jess	Bert	☐ ☆ ☆

Root Beer with Bart.

Bart had said that his shack was smart, for it had a coat of fresh paint, but it was big as well. They went up the stairs and at the top they saw Bart's maid. She had to mop up the muck, and in a dump this can be a hard job.

"You can put Froid's chair here by this pail of snails." said Bart. "Here is the root beer. If you wait, Meg, the maid, will bring you a glass. Then she will put lunch on the oak board by the stairs."

Mark said, "I am not a big boy and my mum says I must not drink much root beer. Can I have a glass of milk?"

Vern said, "I am a big boy and I can drink lots of root beer. Put my glass here. Cheers!"

DECODING ~ POWER ~ PAGE

Some of these words are unusual, but they are all real words.

quick	kerb	rash	fifth	☐
mort	chug	quench	morse	☐
swill	glad	brim	drop	☐
peep	lard	shed	geese	☐
loft	junk	kelp	ink	☐
shack	perch	Seth	pick	☐
brass	grim	spot	swam	☐
pair	shore	deer	oar	☐
tar	baize	tee	noise	☐
sung	jail	wimp	moist	☐

chop   coat   coach

Mum said I should put on my ___.

park   pair   pick

Wait for your gran in the car ___.

oaks   oaths   oats

Would you give the horse some ___?

tamp   tank   tent

We could go and help put up the ___.

soil   sort   socks

Would you give me that pair of your ___?

shed   sheep   shop

My goat lives in that ___.

sham	got	Herb	far	☐ ☆ ☆
buff	buck	fee	nag	☐ ☆ ☆
bath	dish	tod	puck	☐ ☆ ☆
peel	mess	sock	shot	☐ ☆ ☆
teg	seem	duff	berth	☐ ☆ ☆
arm	them	feet	doff	☐ ☆ ☆
kick	card	will	dock	☐ ☆ ☆
shell	fib	her	carp	☐ ☆ ☆
cox	ruck	lash	fid	☐ ☆ ☆

Mark has a bath.

Mark said, "Could I have a bath now? My hair is full of moist muck."

Bart the damp dog said, "Yes, you can go up the stairs and have a bath. Be quick now, or you will miss your lunch."

So Mark went up the stairs. The stairs went up and up. They went up so far that Mark could see the stars in the sky.

At last Mark got to the bath. He got in the hot tub with some soap and had a long soak.

Then he had to wait for Meg the maid, who said, "You cannot put wet socks back on and there is lots of muck on this pair of shorts. Here, let me give you some pink flip-flops to put on for now, and I will lend you a pair of my dad's shorts and a top"

"But I am small boy," Mark said, "not a tall man!" But Mark had to put big shorts and a top or he would have had to go to lunch in just the pink flip-flops.

Mark got back but there was no lunch. Groyne, the grey-green goat, was there. The quiff in his hair was stiff with mud. "Have a munch on this board," he said. Vern, Bart and Froid had drunk all the root beer.

"Give this last glass of root beer to Herb," said Bart, "He cannot come up the stairs, for he is a sharp shark."

Mark had to ask, "How did Herb get here? Has he paid ten quid for a bus pass?"

Mastery Test

If your pupil does not pass this test, they must go back to page 127. This is very important—a child who is struggling will not be learning. Contrary to what you would think, most children would rather go back than carry on getting things wrong. If your pupil needs to go back, use a different coloured pencil for ticking the boxes.

Use the cursor as you would on a Fluency Reading page

Timed reading: 'Pass' mark is 15 seconds per line.

| spark | score | creep | tray | ☐ |

| stern | point | float | quack | ☐ |

| brain | chair | coy | stork | ☐ |

Reading accuracy: Pass mark is one mistake.
Do not prompt. You may allow the pupil to self correct, but you cannot say anything except "Try again".

There is still some corn left in the grain store. ☐

Could you put your coat next to her cloak? ☐

Last week, Joan wore her hair in a braid. ☐

We saw where Roy hid his sports bag. ☐

Clair will paint the boards with a green stain. ☐

This book has been produced in line with the EU GPSR guidelines about the safety of products.

The General Product Safety Regulation is the European Union's updated framework for ensuring that all consumer products, including books, are safe for consumers.

This book has been printed by Libri Plureos GmbH. The printer has issued safety certificates for the materials - like ink, paper and glue - being used.

The product identifier is: 9781905174508

The author is responsible for the content of the book, is the publisher of the works and bears full responsibility for it.

The book has been produced via Bookmundo. Bookmundo enables any author to share their stories with the rest of the world via printed books and ebooks and a broad distribution network.

Bookmundo will act as an intermediary in regard to questions about safety and will address them to the printer / author. Should there be any question in regard to the safety of the product, please contact us.

Bookmundo
Delftsestraat 33
3013AE Rotterdam
The Netherlands
info@bookmundo.com